Poltergeists

Cases and Testimonies of an Entirely Mysterious Paranormal Phenomenon

Conrad Bauer

All rights reserved © 2021 by Conrad Bauer and Maplewood Publishing. No part of this publication or the information in it may be quoted from or reproduced in any form by means such as printing, scanning, photocopying, or otherwise without prior written permission of the copyright holder.

Efforts have been made to ensure that the information in this book is accurate and complete. However, the author and the publisher do not warrant the accuracy of the information, text, and graphics contained within the book due to the rapidly changing nature of science, research, known and unknown facts, and the internet. The author and the publisher do not hold any responsibility for errors, omissions, or contrary interpretation of the subject matter herein. This book is presented solely for motivational and informational purposes only

ISBN 9798777705280

Printed in the United States

Contents

How it Typically Begins — 5

Making Sense of The Bell Witch — 7

Poltergeist on the March — 25

The Battersea Mystery House — 25

Gef the Mongoose Geist — 35

The 28-Day Poltergeist of Virginia Campbell — 41

Anne Marie Schneider's Poltergeist — 47

The Hodgson's and the Enfield Poltergeist — 53

Renate Beck and the Indianapolis Poltergeist — 71

Poltergeists and Skinwalkers — 77

One Noisy Ghost — 87

Further Readings — 90

How it Typically Begins

Right when your back is turned, you could have *sworn* that you just heard the distinct sound of footsteps behind you. Even worse, as you were busy typing on the kitchen table of your home, out of the corner of your eye, you could have *sworn* you saw the cabinet door, ever so slightly, open and close, all of its own accord. These vague manifestations are typically the first phase—the opening salvos if you will—of poltergeist activity.

Like a paranormal snowball rapidly traveling downhill, these paranormal events then transform into more complex ones, such as seeing whole objects levitating, or hearing the murmurings of a voice. That voice is so indistinct and distant at first—distant enough for you to still wonder if your mind is playing tricks on you—then suddenly it starts to form clear and coherent words.

Those words become part of whole sentences, and the next thing you know you are directly communicating with an unseen and hidden intelligence of apparently immense proportions—something for a lack of a better word—we call a "poltergeist." The term is borrowed from German and roughly translates as "noisy ghost."

Yes, they are indeed noisy, attention-getting tricksters, but much *more* than that. The intelligence behind the poltergeist phenomenon seems to know everything about you, as well as everything about others. The classic Bell Witch case is an example of this super-clairvoyance. For in this legendary case of poltergeist happenings, you find a poltergeist entity seemingly able to turn a whole community of local gossips against each other.

Nothing was sacred in the presence of the incessantly chattering, Bell Witch poltergeist. From the Bell Witch to the Skinwalker Ranch—the cases you will read about in this book defy explanation. All of these accounts share one common thread—there are still aspects of our reality which we still don't fully understand. Be prepared to have your mind completely and irrevocably blown!

Making Sense of The Bell Witch

The case of the so-called "Bell Witch" is perhaps one of the most infamous supposed poltergeist cases of all time. The alleged event occurred in the rural confines of Robertson County, Tennessee, sometime between 1817 and 1821. The poltergeist activity erupted on a local farmstead owned by a man named John Bell, in the vicinity of modern-day Adams, Tennessee, near the Kentucky border.

The Bell family consisted of Mr. John Bell, Mrs. Lucy Bell, and their nine kids. It was a hardworking and isolated life on the Bell farm, in which their growing brood of youngsters' days, were usually spent working on the farm, and otherwise in solitude.

Not much was happening in their young lives—that is—not much was happening until 1817 when they began to interact with a powerful poltergeist force of unknown origin.

As is typical in most cases of poltergeist activity, the phenomenon manifested itself gradually, slowly increasing in intensity. The first hints this poltergeist dropped to indicate its presence, was through simply scratching and making pitter-patter sounds in the middle of the night. Since the family lived on a farm in which the entrance of a field mouse or two wasn't all that uncommon, such sounds could be fairly easily ignored or rationalized away.

These bumps in the night, however, began to grow louder and more insistent as the days wore on, and soon graduated from mouse level nuisance, to what seemed like a large animal intruding on the property. Mr. Bell no doubt checked the premises as best he could, but couldn't find any signs of the wild beast that they continually heard stamping about in the middle of the night.

It was the following year, in 1818, that these midnight rumblings took a new turn, because instead of just hearing animal-like scrapes about the property, one fine spring night, they were startled to hear loud knocking, banging, and thrashing about, which sounded like something a *human* intruder might do. Yet no human intruder was found. Even so, these nocturnal intrusions would continue.

Much more distressing, at one point these nightly disturbances began to be accompanied by weird "lip-smacking" sounds. It was as if someone were trying to form words or find their voice, but all they could do was smack their lips. The family was obviously deeply disturbed (who wouldn't be awake to a lip smacker in the middle of the night?) but they could not find any logical explanation for what they were all experiencing.

The lip-smacking then graduated to the sound of someone gurgling or being choked. As disturbing as all of this was, up to this point, all the family was experiencing were these decidedly odd sounds. Soon, however, this force would break through the sound barrier entirely, and begin direct interaction with material objects. Graduating from scratching and lip-smacking, the paranormal beast began to snatch sheets and covers right off the sleeping forms of the Bell children.

How spooky is that, right? As a kid, you might remember that unspoken rule about the boogey man—how he can't get you if you pull the blanket over your head? At least maybe that's what your parents told you. So, one can only imagine how frightening it would be to have an unseen force suddenly pull that sacred security blanket right off!

Just imagine these kids hearing spooky sounds outside and pulling their trusty blanky up over their heads and then—*BAM!*—it comes flying right off! Sure enough, blood-curdling screams ensued, followed perhaps by a few choice words from John Bell, awakened by the terrible commotion in the next room.

The family was pretty darn hysterical at this point, but if having blankets pulled off you in the middle of the night wasn't bad enough, the unseen entity then began to actually put its hands-on members of the Bell family. On one particularly frightening night, one of the Bell boys—Richard—woke up to feel something yanking on his hair. Upon realizing it wasn't one of his siblings tormenting him, but some unseen hand in the darkness, Richard screamed loud enough to wake up the whole house.

Richard's brother Joel experienced the same treatment soon thereafter, and on yet another night, the entity decided to attack their sister Betsy in the same manner. After accosting her, the poltergeist seemed to have made her a favorite, for she was soon complaining of having her hair pulled by the unseen force, just about every night thereafter.

Betsy did indeed become the focal point of much of the happenings shortly thereafter, with other physical manifestations being aimed at her, such as stones suddenly materializing and tossed in her direction. For whatever reason, stone-throwing is actually quite common in poltergeist cases and has been reported for centuries. Stones have been witnessed being individually thrown at people, and in some cases, witnesses outside of poltergeist-afflicted homes, have actually seen stones appear to rain down from the sky.

Young Betsy, too, was seen having stones hurled at her, during the Bell Witch phenomena. As the happenings progressed, it was clear that this poltergeist was increasing in strength, and as such, was able to more forcefully manifest itself into our reality. Soon after the stone-throwing incident, the unseen presence is said to have actually struck Betsy across the face. This incident was witnessed directly by Betsy's brother.

He heard the sound of the slap, saw his sister react as if she had just been physically slapped, and then saw the very real, reddened imprint of the unseen hand that had struck her. Their concerned father John Bell was understandably at his wits' end, and at this point, he decided to involve the neighbors. In particular, he recruited a local guy by the name of James Johnson who was known to be rather studious when it came to religion and biblical scripture.

It was hoped that James could use some of his spiritual knowledge to cast out what was no doubt perceived as a very evil and malignant spirit. Mr. Johnson, however, began to suspect that perhaps Betsy was the one behind the whole thing, and was just playing a bit of make-believe. Never mind the fact that the other children had experienced direct encounters with the entity, Johnson began to speculate that perhaps Betsy was playing games with her family.

Since poltergeists tend to focus on one person, and much of the reported activity occurs in the presence of that said person—such a conclusion is understandable. If crazy stuff only happens when Betsy is in the room, it's rather logical to think that perhaps it's Betsy who's the troublemaker, trying to trick everybody else. But as compelling as such an explanation may be, the fact that most people targeted by this bizarre activity seem genuinely frightened, usually makes witnesses seek answers elsewhere.

It is indeed a common thread in poltergeist cases to have a person fulfill a role, which investigators have dubbed being a "focus" for the poltergeist activity. But that doesn't mean that this individual is engaged in fraud. For those that believe that perhaps poltergeists are uncontrollable manifestations of the subconscious mind, it has been theorized that a "focus" like Betsy may be unknowingly projecting psychokinetic manifestations.

Others have suggested that maybe the poltergeist—whatever type of entity it may be—needs to focus on and feed off of one individual directly, using their victim's own psyche to charge their batteries, and the more charged up the poltergeist gets, the more it can manifest into our world.

As it pertains to the Bell family and their "witch," their neighbor Mr. Johnson was skeptical. But then Mr. Johnson got his own taste of the lip-smacking Bell Witch. He was visiting the house and watching and waiting for any sign of anything untoward when he heard the distinct sound of lip-smacking behind him. Johnson didn't know who or what was causing the disturbance, but he immediately turned around and shouted, "Stop it! In the name of the Lord!"

James Johnson was pleased that the perpetrator did indeed manage to stifle their lip-smacking upon making this declaration. It's said that for the rest of Johnson's visit, all was calm and peaceful in the Bell household. But as soon as this inquisitive neighbor went on his way and left the family to their own machinations, the activity took right off where it left off.

And Betsy began to once again suffer attacks by an unseen force. As the family continued to complain of these strange happenings, kindly neighbor Johnson once again showed up and gave Mr. Bell a piece of advice. He encouraged him to get as many neighbors as possible involved and have them take shifts, watching over the house. It's unclear if Johnson was a true believer in poltergeist activity at this point, or if he simply thought that extra eyes might catch some crafty kids pranking the adults.

At any rate, even after other members of the community became involved, strange happenings in the Bell household continued. Still, there was skepticism among outsiders. That all seemed to change, however, when one vocal neighbor openly expressed his doubts. The man stated that it was his opinion that perhaps it was all just a ploy of Mr. Bell's kids to get attention.

No sooner were the words out of his mouth, than an unseen fist hit the man right in the head. That was enough to make a believer out of this skeptic, and just about anyone else who lived in the vicinity of the Bell's homestead. Apparently seeing someone KO'd by an invisible entity tends to make a believer out of people. It was at this point that the strange tales of the Bell family became the strange tales of an entire community in northern Tennessee.

If reports are to be believed (and of course, that is a big if) the haunting of the Bell farm even expanded to include the surrounding territory. It's said that a dirt road near the farm that led to the church and school that the Bell kids attended, also began to manifest strange, paranormal activity. Locals would report that about 100 yards across from the Bell property, on this dirt road near a patch of trees, pedestrians would be surprised to suddenly have rocks or sticks hurl themselves from the thicket.

Once alerted to this phenomenon, young Joel Bell seemed to have turned a bit of a game out of it. If a stick flew toward him, he would pick it up and toss it back, only for it to immediately hurl itself right out of the wooded thicket once again. As cute as it might be for a youngster to play catch with the friendly neighborhood poltergeist, the adults in the community were fairly alarmed. Because as all good people know, sticks and stones just might break some bones—and an angry poltergeist really could hurt you!

But any subsequent investigation of the thicket provided no rational explanation as to how the sticks and stones were flying forth from the wooded area. Not knowing what else to do, the locals came to accept that something otherworldly was occurring. And proving how daring they were, they decided that the best way to figure out what the unseen entity was, and what it wanted, was to establish direct contact with it.

This dialogue was initiated through basic taps. The neighbors would tap on a table three times, and then the unseen force would tap back somewhere in the house three times. It was quite obvious that *whatever* it was—it was intelligent and able to reason with them. But it was once this basic form of communication had been struck, that the poltergeist seemed to enter a new phase of its existence, actively seeking a more direct means to express itself.

The concerted taps began to be accompanied by what seemed to be the previous lip-smacking sounds. The lip-smacking then progressed to groaning, growling, and then finally incoherent muttering. The muttering at first was just audible enough to hear a faint voice but no one could make out what it was saying. As the poltergeist seemed to gain in power, however, the mutterings began to take the form of actual words, and then whole sentences that could be heard by all.

The climax of which was the entity declaring to all who would listen, "I am a spirit who was once happy. But I have been disturbed and am now unhappy." Was that what all of this was about? Was the Bell family dealing with a spirit whose eternal slumber had been somehow disturbed? Or is that just what this strange entity wanted everyone to believe? As many of the cases in this book will demonstrate, poltergeists are often deceptive tricksters, and it could very well be a case of the latter.

The poltergeist, once gaining a voice, would not shut up. And the things it said were highly abusive to all considered. John Bell would later indicate that he declined to record in writing much of what the entity said because it was either too profane or even too "blasphemous" to be repeated. The entity also appeared to have a grudge against John Bell—or at least it said it did—menacingly stating that it was its mission to torment "Old Jack Bell."

It was at this point, that the unseen force seemed to shift its focus from John Bell's daughter Betsy, and onto John Bell himself. From here on out, this paranormal menace began to regularly kick, punch, and slap the man. As was its penchant, the entity also routinely threw stones at the poor farmer. In the midst of all of this, John woke up one morning unable to open his mouth. It's hard to know whether it was related to the Bell Witch or some other condition, but he had come down with what doctors call "lock jaw."

This condition only added to John's misery, since it prevented him from eating or speaking for long stretches at a time. Eventually, the ghost developed a more complex backstory for itself, claiming that in life it had been a member of a Native American tribe, whose bones had been buried in the region long ago, only to be disturbed when the Bell family built their homestead on top of the burial site.

The idea of angry spirits emanating from disturbed Native American burial grounds is indeed a long-held trope in hauntings. Considering the age of this particular account, perhaps many of these themes can be traced back to the tale of the Bell Witch. But even the Bell Witch entity itself, couldn't stick to this story, because shortly after uttering it, the poltergeist suddenly changed its mind and declared that its true identity was that of "Old Kate Batt's Witch." Whatever that means, right?

Actually, according to legend, Kate Batts was a midwife who lived in the region. Since Kate Batt was a real person in the community, the Bell Witch was essentially calling her out, by claiming to be her familiar spirit—or "witch." By proclaiming "Hey! I'm old Kate Batt's witch!" The poltergeist was casting deep suspicion on one of the Bell's own neighbors.

This, of course, led to Kate herself being questioned. She was shocked to hear of the accusations that this disembodied spirit had leveled against her and denied all charges. It would later become clear that this poltergeist trickster was absolutely thrilled in concocting schemes to tear this community apart. If the *Bell Witch* could get these locals at each other's throats so easily, one can't help but wonder if perhaps a couple of centuries prior in a colonial town in Massachusetts, if a *Salem Witch* poltergeist was able to do the same?

At any rate, before they began to kill each other over false accusations, the community had to get wise and realize that the Bell Witch was just making up rubbish to get the community in an uproar. And when the plot to sow discord didn't work quite as the entity had planned, it decided to change things up a bit, by producing even more unseen personalities.

Soon a new voice was added to the mix—the voice of a man, who called himself "Black Dog." Soon thereafter, there could also be heard the sound of a little boy, and a woman. These voices began to pal around together like the best of poltergeist friends. They are said to have sung "drinking songs" and entertained each other by cracking crass jokes.

These lively "spirits" if you will, were said to be so rambunctious, that they feigned intoxication by way of emitting a strong odor of alcohol. At this point, you're probably kicking yourself thinking—if only they had the technology back then to make some audio recordings of this poltergeist booze binge! Well—as we will see in some of the more modern tales—even if they did that, it might not have made much of a difference.

Because in modern cases that deal with these poltergeist tricksters, they seem to have the habit of interfering with electronics and rendering them absolutely useless as it pertains to capturing their activity. And as skeptics will happily point out, this is also the perfect excuse for fraudsters, as to why they never catch anything on tape! If someone was just perpetuating a fraud and asked for proof—they could say there is no proof, because the poltergeist destroyed the evidence.

In the midst of all of this Bell Witch supposed poltergeist revelry, the disembodied voices began to meddle in local affairs by revealing the problems of the locals, in a very forthright and—at least for those involved—humiliating fashion. The fact that this entity was able to project its perception into households both near and far, to pick up on these details, made it a very frightening force to be reckoned with.

For much more frightening than the banging, the knocking, and even the slaps to the face, where the intimate details of the townspeople's daily lives were suddenly put on full display. This entity was apparently able to reveal the deepest darkest secrets, as well as long-held animosities of those in that small, rural Tennessee community. Some of the townspeople must have been somewhat drawn to this force and its clairvoyant ability.

The entity at times even feigned interest in improving the lot in life of some of the locals. As was the case when it claimed to have knowledge of a buried treasure. The Bell children took the entity very seriously when it told them if they dug in a certain spot on the property, they would strike gold. They did as they were instructed, spending quite a long time, sweating and laboring to dig up the earth. Worn out and weary from the exertion they eventually gave up and returned home.

Upon their return, the entity immediately broke into laughter and began mocking them for falling for its apparent ruse. There was no treasure! The poltergeist simply wanted to have a little fun at their expense. But the entity was, by far, most aggressive with John Bell. And on one particular occasion, the entity proved especially malicious. It's said that Mr. Bell had just stepped outside to get some fresh air when the unseen force took hold of his feet.

Try as he might move forward, the entity's rock-solid grip prevented him from taking another step. Then all of a sudden, the entity let go. John Bell no doubt relieved to be free, stepped forward, only to be punched in the face. The unseen force hit John in the jaw like a sledgehammer, causing him to fall backward. He ended up landing on a nearby log, where he sat for a moment, trying to regain his wits. The poltergeist wasn't done with John Bell, however, and proceeded to lift him off the log and toss him to the side like a rag doll.

As John struggled to get away, the Bell Witch supposedly began to pull him by the hands and feet, yanking him about, as he helplessly lay on the ground. The poltergeist eventually became bored of playing with its prey, however, and let John go. John was free to get up and walk, but he wasn't free of the poltergeist's taunts as the disembodied voice continued to make a mockery of him—serenading him with "offensive songs."

John was eventually helped inside by his son Richard, who helped lead his battered and bruised father to bed. But although the poltergeist was particularly cruel to John Bell, it was downright friendly to his wife

Lucy Bell. In stark contrast to how it treated everyone else, the poltergeist would often say kind things about Lucy. And on one occasion when she was sick, the poltergeist felt sorry for her and wished to cheer her up. It tried to do so, by materializing a tasty snack—hazelnuts—right out of thin air, having them suddenly just pop into existence in her sick bed.

Upon seeing the nuts, Lucy happened to remark, "Oh, but we have no nutcrackers." Instead of materializing a nutcracker so she could crack the nuts, this charming little Geist, simply materialized a whole "two pounds" of already cracked hazelnuts right in front of the sick lady, so she could munch on them to her heart's content.

As sweet as this gesture was, unfortunately for John Bell, (he was definitely on the bad side of this split personality poltergeist), and according to the legend of the Bell Witch, this would cost him his very life. It was in the early evening hours of the 18th of December, in 1820, that this besieged patriarch told his family that he was going to bed because he felt like he needed to rest. Little did his family know at the time—he wouldn't wake up from his slumber.

The next day in fact, when he was found dying, in an apparent comatose state, the poltergeist announced with glee, "It's useless for you to try to relieve Old Jack. I've got him this time. He will never get up from that bed again." It was then that Mr. Bell's son John Jr. happened to lay his eyes on what looked like a vial of some kind of liquid. It was then that the poltergeist confirmed, "I put it there. And I gave Old Jack a dose last night while he was asleep, which fixed him."

Mr. Bell is said to have perished the next day, from whatever poison the poltergeist had got him to drink. On the day of Mr. Bell's funeral, the poltergeist was heard marching around the Bell home and singing old "drinking songs" with glee. The case of the Bell Witch stands out because it's one of the only known cases in which a poltergeist actually killed someone.

There are those, however, who would argue that none of these things happened at all. And even though there is a land marker in Tennessee to mark the supposed site of the Bell property and where all of these horrific things supposedly transpired—some say that this story is simply a legend that got out of control. The jury may still be out on the veracity of the Bell Witch—but it's a riveting tale of the supposed supernatural all the same.

And what supposedly happened to the Bell Witch? According to the narrative that's been passed down, shortly after Mr. Bell's death, the poltergeist manifested a cannonball and had it roll down the chimney, only to stop in the middle of the family home. The cannonball then exploded into a smoky haze, as the Bell Witch announced, "I am going and will be gone for seven years."

According to legend, it did indeed return seven years later, but the Bell family chose to actively ignore the poltergeist, and by doing so it either lost interest or literally lost its ability to manifest. For once the family decided to give the poltergeist the cold shoulder, and refused to acknowledge it—the poltergeist allegedly ceased to exist of its own accord.

Robinson heard the same telltale pitter-pattering once again.

Robinson was ready this time and immediately rushed outside to see if he could find the source of the disturbance. But as soon as he emerged from the home, the phenomenon ceased, and there was no one to be seen. Robinson figured whoever was doing it must have been awful quick on their feet. Robinson wasn't going to give up, however, and shortly thereafter, when this phenomenon occurred again, both he and his visiting nephew Peter, rushed out to catch the supposed prankster.

They didn't see anyone, but about as soon as they got outside, they heard the terrible sound of shattering glass. Upon returning inside, they discovered that the glass panels in the roof had been pulverized by a huge lump of coal that had slammed right through it like a meteorite. This was no meteor, however; it was simply plain coal, that had mysteriously rained down on all the other occasions.

This family did not even possess a phone in those days, so the disturbed Mr. Robinson had his nephew run off on foot to bring him a police officer. Peter came back with a police officer on hand to take a look at the place. The policeman assuming that this was some sort of instance of vandalism, did his best to take down witness statements from Robinson and Peter. Robinson and the police officer then went outside to talk further.

Poltergeist on the M: The Battersea Mystery House

It was on the 29th of November in 1928, tha the name of Frederick Robinson was mindir business, hanging out in the dining room of London home, when something really weird happening. He heard a kind of "pitter-patter" the roof. The first thing that might come to m hearing such a sound is perhaps a few raind striking the roof.

But it wasn't forecast to rain that day. Curiou Robinson went over to his conservatory, whe had a section of glass paneling on the ceiling which he could gaze upward. He was then in shock. For he looked up just in time to see wl appeared to be bits of coal raining down on th As soon as it had begun, however, the pheno appeared to subside, leaving Robinson to wo how in the world coal could rain down on his h

Short of some freak of nature—Robinson was sure that there must be some kind of local pra somewhere, playing a game with him. Neverth he didn't need coal on his roof, so he went out hopped up on a ladder, and cleared the debris was a few days later on December 2nd, that Mr

They then heard the sound of something hitting the roof of the house. To both their shock, they looked up to see what appeared to be pennies falling from the clouds! Upon seeing this odd phenomenon, the policeman knew the objects weren't being thrown. If they had been, they would have proceeded with an "arc." An object thrown onto the roof from nearby would have to have been launched from the ground, up high into the air, and then arc back down on top of the roof. But this is not what happened.

The two men saw with their own eyes, pennies dropping straight down from above as if the heavens suddenly began raining them. As strange as all of these happenings were, they were just the very beginning of a whole odd series of poltergeist-styled events that would occur in and around this otherwise quiet and unsuspecting London home.

Objects began to move of their own volition, and strange voices were heard. The manifestations then became even bolder on the evening of December 19th, when a maid who worked for the family was in the household laundry room. She entered the room to wash clothes, only to find a whole pile of coals actually lit up and on fire, right in front of her.

The door to the room was locked, and the maid and Frederick were the only two equipped with keys to unlock it. Nevertheless, Frederick was immediately summoned, so that he too could puzzle over this bizarre sight. It was just a few days later when the whole house was rocked at 9 in the morning when loud banging and crashing sounds were suddenly being emitted at random from just about every corner of the house.

If you can imagine it, the situation was like suddenly waking up to the sounds of a construction crew hammering away right in your living room—yet not finding a trace of anyone or anything there—just the sounds of the crew hammering away. Even worse, however, happened shortly thereafter—one of the windows of the elderly Mr. Robinson's room suddenly blew to pieces right in front of him.

It appeared as if someone had hurled a stone at the glass window, yet there was no such perpetrator—nor was there even a stone to recover. It was as if some entirely invisible object had shattered the windowpane. Frederick was worried for his frail father's own safety at this point and actually asked a neighbor—Mr. Bradbury—if the elder Robinson could stay with him. Bradbury agreed and came over to pick the old man up.

It was as the elder Robinson was departing with Bradbury that more objects in the house began to move of their own accord. At one point a "heavy chest" began to rock, before slamming down on the floor. Then right when Bradbury and the elder Robinson were making their exit, a hat stand by the front door began to move around as if it suddenly had a life of its own.

Frederick tried to seize the hat stand, but as soon as he made the attempt, the stand was ripped from his grasp by an apparently unseen entity. The unseen force then apparently hurled the hat stand with all of its might, causing it to slam into the stairs, and actually break in half. Frederick was understandably at a loss and had no way to explain what was happening to him and his family in what had otherwise been a happy home.

It was all of these happenings, that led a paranormal investigator by the name of Harry Price to the residence at Battersea, on January 19th, 1929. Upon his arrival at the residence, everything seemed normal enough. He found the 86-year-old head of the house—Henry Robinson, at the table with his four grown kids—Lillah, Frederick, Kate, and Mary—finishing up what had been their morning meal.

Mary whose married name was Perkins was a recent widow who had moved back in with her Dad, along with her 14-year-old son Peter. Peter, of course, was the boy who was present with his uncle, Frederick Robinson at the initial outset of this very strange activity. It was Frederick who got up from the family table that day and took the lead, introducing himself to Price and then showing him around the home.

He led Price into the conservatory room of the house and showed him the broken glass, as well as sites of other disturbances. After this brief tour, he told Price that he, as well as his adult sisters, would have to leave for work, and Peter would have to head off to class. Nevertheless, Price was intrigued and requested to be able to return later on.

Harry Price did indeed return, later that day, he was also accompanied by a journalist who comes down to us simply as "Mr. Grice" for the "London Evening News." It was Mr. Grice's job to take notes should anything unusual occur. Grice took note of the destruction that had occurred in the house. He surveyed the wreckage of several busted windows, dented doors, and other smashed and shattered objects.

Both Price and Grice were impressed with what they saw, and the following day Grice mentioned the odd happenings of the Battersea House in the newspaper. At this point, no one could quite make head nor tail of what was happening, but one commonality did emerge. The vast bulk of the damage had occurred in and around the backside of the house.

This is where most of the windows were smashed and where some of the most spectacular paranormal activity had occurred. Grice did his homework and figured out that directly behind the Robinsons' house was a nursing home for World War One veterans suffering from PTSD, or as it was known then shellshock. It was an interesting aside, but at first glance relatively meaningless.

In the coming days, however, Grice would find that the connection between the suffering souls of this veteran's home and the activity at the Battersea

House, just might run deeper than anyone could have imagined at the time. The first suggestion of a connection was a simple one—Grice inquired with the family if perhaps one of the patients at the home behind them, could be throwing objects at the home.

But since the idea that anyone was throwing objects with such force, and at such angles, had already been ruled out, the suggestion didn't get much traction. Nevertheless, Grice decided to go to the veteran's home himself, and tell the superintendent to keep an eye out for any potential pranksters among those under his care. The situation within the family home of the Robinsons had taken a turn for the worse in the meantime.

Frederick himself suffered a mental breakdown, and after creating a disturbance was taken into police custody. The police at this point, had become convinced that they had found the source of all the strange happenings at the Battersea House—they believed it was Frederick who was causing all of the chaos and confusion. Frederick was ultimately detained in a psych ward and placed under examination.

In the meantime, the police kept a watch on the Battersea House. Despite the prejudice of the responding officers, as it turns out, the extrication of Frederick from the home, did absolutely nothing to alter the startling effects of this poltergeist. Even with Frederick absent, the strange sounds, the moving of objects, and the raining of debris continued unabated—and the most bizarre event was still to come.

For one fine Saturday when Mary Perkins was attempting to straighten up the dining room table, the chairs suddenly pulled out from under the table of their own accord. Startled, Mrs. Perkins began to back away. It was then that the chairs moved into a line and began to march in single file as if they were soldiers. Perkins began running to the stairs at this point and was quite relieved that the chair force didn't follow.

Instead, they simply turned around and marched back to the dining room. By the time she dared to peek back into the dining room, she then found the previously marching chairs, all stacked on top of the table. Mary Perkins—perhaps showing more bravery than most—then proceeded to unstack the chairs and put them back under the table. She then left the room, and came back just a short time later, only to find the chairs stacked back on the table once again.

She then put them back one more time, but once again, moments later, they were again back on top of the table. Although you might think that the marching chairs would have been enough, this was apparently when Perkins finally lost it and ran outside to get the police. One officer who had been watching the place from outside joined her in the dining room, but he didn't believe her story. Prompting a frustrated Mrs. Perkins to bid the man farewell.

It was on the following evening that Kate Robinson would have her turn of odd events. She was minding her own business doing her morning chores, when a suitcase belonging to her brother, suddenly flew from one side of the kitchen to the other, almost hitting her in the process. She took off running, but once she reached the hall, she was greeted by a floating umbrella. She then made her way back to the kitchen and found her nephew Peter standing there amid chairs, that seemed to be rocking back and forth.

As they stood and watched, the whole kitchen table then flipped onto the floor. Absolutely terrified, the two ran right out of the house. Once out the door, they could then clearly see through the window, that the chairs were dancing and moving about the kitchen floor. They did this for a few moments before knocking themselves over and coming to a stop. The house was a horrific mess and soon its residents no longer wished to call it home.

Kate and Mary left, and shortly thereafter Peter was sent off to a relative for his own safety. It was while Peter was gone that the activity in the home suddenly came to a stop. Frederick was released from police custody a short time later and returned to the house. So did Kate and Mary. But it was right around this time that the elderly Mr. Robinson passed away.

It was after the passing of their father, that his adult children decided to leave the home for good, and rented a place of their own. No one quite knows what to make of this story to this very day. The easiest explanation for those who do not wish to delve into the paranormal aspect would be that folks' imaginations simply ran away with them. But unless witnesses were outright lying about what they saw—there is no real way that one could imagine things such as chairs marching in single file.

As it pertains to the poltergeist theory, however, there seem to be two possible explanations. Since the activity ended after Peter was removed from the home, it would seem that Peter was the focus of this poltergeist's activity. Another element of the story however is the veteran's home, which most certainly housed individuals who were suffering from troubled mental conditions.

They too could have somehow been a focal point of an immense outpouring of poltergeist activity. And the story of the chairs marching like soldiers really does make one consider that possibility. The mystery of the Battersea House remains unsolved.

Gef the Mongoose Geist

Perhaps the most bizarre alleged poltergeist account is that of a friendly little Geist named Gef. Proving that poltergeists can take all kinds of forms, Gef presented himself to the family he haunted as a talking mongoose. And since this writer for one, had no clue what in fact a mongoose was prior to writing this piece—let's go ahead and clear that up first: A mongoose is a small furry animal related to the meerkat.

Basically, a rambunctious little cat-like critter who runs on all fours but can also stand up on two feet and use their hands a bit like us humans do. Now that this has been established, let's delve into the escapades of Gef the Mongoose Geist. This case begins in 1931, at a remote (isn't it always remote?) country home, on the Isle of Man. For readers perhaps not familiar with the geography, the Isle of Man is an island, just west of Britain and east of Ireland.

It was here, at the rural homestead of James and Margaret Irving, that a most bizarre poltergeist made itself known. It was their daughter Voirrey, who seemed to be the initial focus of this manifestation when she was just 13 years of age. Mr. Irving was a little older than his wife Margaret, and after a successful career in sales, he had gone into retirement and purchased the old homestead on the Isle of Man.

They knew it was a real "fixer-upper" but with a bit of love, and a little hard work they figured they would survive. Voirrey in the meantime was an inquisitive child, and due to a lack of playmates, often sought the company of the little animals that made their way onto the property. Perhaps it was for this very reason that the poltergeist manifested itself to her… as a mongoose!

As was typically the case, the occurrences began gradually. First, the family began to hear what they took for the "scurrying" of animals outside the walls of the house. These sounds were then accompanied by growls and other animalesque vocalizations. But this wasn't the end of it. For soon the family began to experience odd tremors as if the whole home was shaking.

This was certainly not normal, yet the family still entertained the idea that their experience was simply from some animal flitting about outside their home. James Irving, intrigued by the phenomenon, attempted to make various animal calls to see if he could get a response. To his surprise, he *did*. And whatever it was perfectly imitated whatever animal call he made. If he imitated a hedgehog, he received back a perfect imitation of a hedgehog, if he imitated a fox, he heard fox calls sent right back, and the same for birds, and any other animal imitation.

But things would become very strange when the animal sounds began to become words. These words then developed into whole conversations. It was at this point that the entity claimed that it was a mongoose who hailed from India. The entity also apparently once spouted off the words, "I am a freak. I have hands and I have feet, and if you saw me, you'd faint, you'd be petrified, mummified, turned into stone or a pillar of salt!"

Well—when you say it like that if this entity's true form is really that frightening, perhaps they were better off *not* seeing it as it really was. You could almost imagine someone responding to the poltergeist, *"Hey! Do you want to pretend you're a mongoose rather than a shockingly frightening monstrosity? Okay, sure! I'll go with the mongoose!"*

As absurd as all this sounds, the family took the talking mongoose (which no one had actually seen) at its word, as its disembodied voice continued to regularly speak with them. At some point, the family managed to get a hold of a paranormal investigator named Harry Price. Yes—this is the same Harry Price mentioned earlier in this book, who was involved with the Battersea Mystery House.

It was Price who referred the family to a fellow investigator whose name comes down to us as "Captain MacDonald." Mr. MacDonald showed up at Irving's home on February 26th, 1932. MacDonald hung out with the family for a few hours but didn't notice anything out of the ordinary.

He then got up and announced that he had to go. It was as soon as he got up to leave that Gef the poltergeist suddenly revealed itself, shouting, "Go away!"

The poltergeist then apparently thought out loud in regard to the visiting MacDonald, asking, "Who is that man?" The whole house was then suddenly full of all kinds of low-voiced murmuring coming from the poltergeist. MacDonald was amazed, but he really did have to go, and parted company shortly thereafter.

He came back the following evening, however, and as soon as he entered the home, he was privileged to see a fountain of some sort of liquid squirting from the living room wall. The family remarked that this was just a part of the mongoose's normal routine—was the animal supposedly relieving itself from the other side of the wall? And perhaps the greater question was—*why were these people okay with that?*

The poltergeist began to speak to Margaret, and Macdonald attempted to cut in, only for the mongoose to bluntly tell him, "I don't like you." The poltergeist continued to speak with Margaret when she was upstairs, and at one point MacDonald tried to quietly walk up the stairs, to see if he could bear witness to anything. But as soon as he drew near, he heard the poltergeist shout, "He's coming!"

Gef the mongoose then grew quiet and refused to emerge while Macdonald was there. In the Spring of 1932 in the meantime, a friend of the family—Charles Northwood—came by and managed to carry on an independent conversation with the unseen entity.

Everything seemed to be going fine, but when Charles happened to mention that he would like to bring along his boy Arthur so that he too could marvel at the majesty of the talking mongoose, Gef threw a fit.

For reasons only known to the poltergeist, the disembodied voice began to order, "Tell Arthur not to come! He doesn't believe. I won't speak if he does come." Even worse the poltergeist became downright hostile, as it randomly shouted, "I'll blow his brains out with a thrupenny cartridge."

This sheer aggression coupled with the precise descriptors used made the poltergeist's threats bizarre and chilling. Would this unseen entity have carried through with its threat? At any rate, Mr. Northwood certainly wasn't going to take any chances and found a reason to excuse himself from the Irvings' home, shortly thereafter.

It was shortly after this episode, that Gef the poltergeist apparently decided to take up a more permanent residence inside a "wooden box" located in little Voirrey Irving's room. No one actually *saw* this poltergeist varmint mind you, it's just that its disembodied voice was heard emanating from this box.

But although he remained invisible, the poltergeist did more than just talk. He also began to regularly interact with physical objects. It's said he played with a ball, rearranged furniture, slammed doors, and even occasionally lit a match or two. Perhaps the most alarming antics of this poltergeist, however, was his supposed penchant for killing rabbits it found around the property and then dropping off the rabbit carcass right in front of family members.

But this act was not interpreted as a malicious one by the Irving family, on the contrary, they thought Gef was being a helpful little hunter since they would then take the rabbit and store it for meat. In return for the favor, the family would often leave food out for the poltergeist, who—when no one was looking—supposedly ate the treats left for him. The poltergeist is said to have especially liked chocolate and bacon.

At any rate, this poltergeist began to slow down over the next several months, and by 1936 all activity had ceased. Gef the Mongoose had made its exit as inexplicably as it had made its entrance. The family later moved away from the house that hosted all of this strange activity and never heard another word from Gef again.

The new resident, however, would shoot a weasel-like creature shortly after his arrival, and upon being filled in on the Gef story, went to the local paper claiming to have "killed Gef." The Irving family was unconvinced. But nevertheless, they never did hear from that "talking mongoose" ever again.

The 28-Day Poltergeist of Virginia Campbell

In 1960, a small quiet town in Scotland called Sauchie was put on the map by the spectacle of a poltergeist. For it was here that a little girl named Virginia Campbell—just 11 years of age—became the center of a sudden paranormal storm of startling events.

Prior to moving to Sauchie, Virginia had lived with her parents in Donegal, Ireland. Her mother Annie split up with her father, however, prompting her to move over to Scotland to live with some extended family members.

The divorce of her parents was a tough thing for this child to go through. She not only lost regular contact with her father but was also uprooted from her familiar stomping grounds and forced to live in unfamiliar surroundings with unfamiliar people. In the cramped conditions of her new home, she also found herself having to sleep in the same bedroom with her cousin Margaret, who was 9 years old at the time.

This cramped bedroom with cousin Margaret became the center stage of poltergeist activity. The first sign that all was not well occurred on the evening of November 22nd, just after the two cousins were about to go to sleep. Just before they were about to drift off to slumber, they both consciously bore witness to what clearly sounded like a kind of big ball being bounced up and down in the darkened room.

At night our senses are heightened, and in a dark room, our hearing is especially sharp. The mind can easily recognize signature sounds such as doors creaking open or footsteps—and yes, a ball being bounced across a wooden floor is not something that most would miss. Both girls cried out in astonishment at what they were hearing. But when Virginia's mother Annie came up to see what all of the commotions was about—but whoever or whatever was bouncing that ball, abruptly stopped.

From then on, however, the activity only progressed further. For once this unseen entity had the girls' attention, it wasn't going to lose its captive audience. And the next night, it was sure to conduct even further mischief.

Once again as they were about to drift off to sleep, they heard a distinct and unnerving commotion. This time, rather than a ball being bounced, they heard the unmistakable sound of furniture being dragged across the floor.

The dragging of objects across a floor is pretty common in poltergeist cases and even just hauntings in general. One only has to think of the classic trope of a ghost dragging chains across an attic floor, and they get the idea. But what these frightened little girls were hearing wasn't in the attic, it was actually right by the foot of their bed—and it was about to get worse. For soon, the noises graduated to the actual movement of tangible objects.

The girls were startled awake by doors that randomly opened and shut of their own accord. This alarming activity also began to take place at all hours of the day—not just at night. The one main constant to all of this bizarre phenomenon, however, was that it only happened when Virginia was in the vicinity. If Virginia was away from the house, all was quiet—but upon her arrival, the poltergeist activity would start.

Virginia would appear to be that classic "focus" element of a poltergeist event. She was the eye of this paranormal storm, with the winds of this supernatural force spiraling out from her at the center. Her increasingly alarmed relatives, unsure of what to do, called in the local priest to have him pray for an end to the odd happenings. But the prayers did not seem to stop the strange phenomenon. In fact, rather than being isolated to just the home, the paranormal activity actually began to manifest in other locations where Virginia was present. This led to quite a startling event at Virginia's school.

It was her homeroom teacher—a certain Miss Stewart—who was the first person outside Virginia's family to bear witness to this anomaly. At one point the teacher was looking straight ahead at her class when a student—it just so happens, the student who sat right in front of Virginia—stood up from her desk to hand her some classwork. Nothing odd about that.

Just the mundane routine of a student handing over work to their teacher.

But it was as soon as the student stood up that the teacher could have sworn that she saw the child's desk float a few inches off the ground. It apparently hovered for just a moment before gently lowering back down. Such a thing is strange for sure, but it's so random, so quick, and so minor (at least paranormally speaking) that one could easily brush it off as simply their mind playing tricks on them.

And that's precisely what Miss Stewart did. Just imagine the teacher of this class, early in the morning, shaking her head, and thinking, "Wow—I need to get another cup of coffee!"

But soon, the paranormal activity in the classroom would manifest in such a dramatic and obvious fashion, that it could no longer be dismissed as sleepiness or early morning imagination. For it was just a couple of days later, that the teacher happened to notice Virginia acting strangely. The child seemed to be pressing down on the top of her desk as if she were trying to hold it down. The teacher was suspicious, so she called the child out on it.

This prompted Virginia to look up and momentarily become distracted from her previous efforts to press down on the desk. It was as soon as she let go, that the desk top (this was an old school wooden desk with a top that opened up in which books and school supplies could be stored) seemed to open right up, all of its own accord. Virginia, just as startled as everyone else, quickly closed the top of her desk.

This time, her teacher knew that she had seen something very odd, but she wasn't quite sure what to make of it. Was Virginia somehow playing a prank on them? She called Virginia up to her desk, to question her about the whole thing.

The teacher's desk was a huge, old-fashioned hefty wooden desk that normally would take a couple of strong individuals to move from one side of the room to the other. It came as quite a shock, when Virginia stood at her side, that the desk suddenly rose right off the floor of its own accord.

As she spoke with Virginia, the desk began to suddenly rock back and forth. As the entire startled classroom watched, the rocking desk then went airborne, floating up into the air. The startled teacher not knowing what else to do tried to pull the desk back down to the floor but was unable to do so. She then let go and backed away, only for the desk to float up even more. Near the ceiling now, the desk then started to rotate.

After spinning around, the desk then gently dropped back down to the ground. The shocked teacher unsure of what was happening locked eyes with little Virginia, at which Virginia broke into tears, crying, "I'm not doing it! Miss please! Miss! Honest! I'm not!" Putting her own frazzled nerves to the side for a moment, the teacher did her best to soothe the upset child.

It was during the course of this conversation that Miss Stewart was told by upset Virginia, that similar poltergeist phenomena had been occurring for several weeks at home. Even so, Virginia wanted to make it clear that it wasn't she who was causing all of these strange happenings. The teacher then had the job of calming down the rest of the class who were now convinced that they had a ghost on their hands. She dismissed the idea of a ghost, and simply assured the classroom, "So long as I stay here, you are alright."

The activity ramped up even further at Virginia's home in the meantime, with objects randomly moving of their own accord. The entity even began to become physically aggressive against people, with Virginia and Margaret experiencing the sensation of someone "pinching" them as they slept.

Interestingly enough, Virginia's mother Annie kept a close journal of all of these happenings, and it would later be realized that the events seemed to gradually pick up speed over a period of 28 days. The events were minor on the first day of this period and then became violently active on the 28th day. Fortunately for this family, the poltergeist activity—whatever the cause may have been—ceased altogether after a few months.

Anne Marie Schneider's Poltergeist

Most poltergeist cases occur in the home when things go "bump" in the night. But this isn't *always* the case. As is indicated by the poltergeist account of Anne Marie Schneider, who had her poltergeist manifest at the office in which she worked. Anne Marie Schneider worked at a law office in Bavaria, Germany in 1967. The lead attorney that she worked for was a guy by the name of Sigmund Adam.

It was Mr. Adam who first realized that things were out of whack when suddenly his phone lines in the law office would become inoperable for no apparent reason. For a busy law firm, needing to take calls, this was a major problem. Adding to this nuisance, was the fact that when the phones did work, they would often ring for no apparent reason, with no one on the other end. Sigmund Adam was getting pretty sick of these phantom calls, and wondered who the culprit might be.

Things took an even more bizarre turn, however, when not just one phantom call erupted, but several. In fact, every single phone in the whole law office began ringing off the hook. This led to a panicked Sigmund actually calling in a technician named Siemens to come in and take a look at the phones. The phones had stopped ringing at that point, and a dumbfounded Siemens could find no reason why they might ring by themselves.

Nevertheless, he had a job to do, so he went ahead and replaced some components, hoping that would make everyone happy. But shortly after Siemens' departure, the phones began ringing of their own accord once again. This led to Siemens making a return visit to the law office. This time around, he determined that perhaps there might be something wrong with the outside phone line. This led the tech to replace the outside lines, as well as set up a new meter, that would be able to monitor all incoming and outgoing calls.

This meter would prove important because it would be able to track the poltergeist-made phone calls. The meter clearly documented the phones going crazy, even after hours when no one was in the law office, and no one should have been calling. What was happening? That was certainly the number one question burning through Sigmund Adam's mind. Things would only escalate from here when in late October of 1967, not only did Sigmund have to deal with phantom calls but also phantom light bulbs that seemed to switch on and off by themselves.

On October 20th in fact, every single light in the law office suddenly extinguished itself for no apparent reason. This led to yet another technician—this time for the lights—to be summoned over, to take a look at the bulbs. The tech found a simple solution to the problem. He screwed the light bulbs back in place.

The lights you see had all somehow unscrewed from their sockets just enough to cause them to go out. Light bulbs, of course, don't normally unscrew themselves.

The only natural explanation that could possibly even come close to explaining such a phenomenon would be if the building had been hit with violent tremors from an earthquake, which could have shaken the bulbs loose. But there was no earthquake in Bavaria, Germany on October 20th, 1967. And even if there had been, the odds that the tremors of such a quake could successfully dislodge every single light bulb in the office all at once, are so remote—it's absurd to even consider.

Yet just moments after the electrician screwed the bulbs back in place, they all suddenly went out again. There was no earthquake that day—but something very unusual was most certainly occurring. And it kept occurring. One month later on November 20th, in fact, that poltergeist reached a new milestone in the office by not only unscrewing the standard bulbs but also somehow detaching the "fluorescent tube" of the fluorescent lighting in Sigmund Adam's own personal office. The tube had come entirely undone, and dropped right from the ceiling, shattering into a thousand pieces with a terrific crash, when it hit the floor below.

The next day, even more trouble was in store when the photocopying machine abruptly began to empty itself of the chemicals stored inside of it. Shortly thereafter, the office began to have trouble with its lighting once again. But instead of the lights simply going out, they began to all explode one by one, causing the glass to fly everywhere. Sigmund was then alarmed to see a hanging chandelier sway from side to side. The distressed Sigmund cynically remarked, "All we need now is for the paintings to move."

Then, as if on cue, a large painting on the wall began to actually rotate around the peg that supported it. Other objects also began to move about at this point. If there were any doubters left to the paranormal nature of what they were experiencing—at this point they became believers. Nevertheless, the disturbed lawyer actually filed a police report. It remains unclear how the cops might bust a poltergeist, but the police trying to remain rational in their investigation pursued the angle that a former client or colleague was somehow behind the disturbances as a means to get back at Sigmund.

This change of tack led the police to pay attention to a young clerk who worked at the office, by the name of Anne Marie Schneider. Ms. Schneider was unassuming enough, but the detectives on the case found that she was very dissatisfied with the job, and did not get along well with Sigmund at all. Even more importantly, the detective on the case found that the main disturbances seemed to occur when Anne Marie was present. In order to test this, the detective suggested that Sigmund give the staff a day off from work, each one getting their time off on different days of the week.

Sure enough, when it came to be Anne Marie's turn to have to time off, nothing unusual happened while she was away from the office. Yet, upon her return, the strange activity ratcheted up once again. The detectives thought they found a clear connection, but rather than considering the paranormal, they believed that Anne Marie was actively sabotaging the office. They just didn't know-how.

Then while two police officers were present, several people in the office witnessed a large "oak cabinet" slide from one side of the office to the other. Never mind the fact that furniture shouldn't move by itself, this particular piece of office furnishing was so heavy, that even the two burly police officers present, had a hard time pushing it back where it had come from. For the detectives on duty, it finally became clear that this was no hoax—something very unusual really was occurring.

It was around this time that the case came to the attention of a so-called "parapsychologist" by the name of Hans Bender. Mr. Bender debriefed on the happenings, took Anne Marie under his wing, and began to test her for any possible latent psychic abilities. Despite all of his efforts, however, Bender could not conclude that Anne Marie had extrasensory powers to speak of.

It was shortly after this, that Sigmund, unsure of what else he could possibly do, had Anne Marie fired. If Anne Marie had filed for unemployment, it must have been quite interesting when she filled out the section of the form that inquired about the reason for termination. Perhaps she declared, *"I was fired because of a poltergeist!"* One can only wonder!

At any rate, it was after her firing that all strange activity in Sigmund's law office ceased. It seems that Anne Marie had some deep misgivings about her workplace, and they boiled to the surface by way of a poltergeist. Having that said, it probably really was best for all involved that she and Sigmund's law firm parted company.

The Hodgson's and the Enfield Poltergeist

In the London suburb of Enfield, the residence on Green Street appeared normal from the outside. Yet little did anyone know of the paranormal drama that was unfolding within these walls. The head of the household was a single mother named Peggy Hodgson. Mrs. Hodgson was a middle-aged woman, recently separated from her husband, and seeking a new start in life, while having her hands entirely full with her four children.

Peggy Hodgson was barely getting by through child support from her ex-husband, coupled with whatever social assistance programs she qualified for. Nevertheless, Peggy Hodgson did her best to put on a brave face, and she was known as being warm and polite to those who encountered her. As mentioned, Peggy Hodgson had four kids to raise—11-year-old Janet, 13-year-old Margaret, seven-year-old Billy, and ten-year-old Johnny.

Adding to her troubles, little Johnny was recovering from cancer, and often away from the house for treatment. There was a lot of tension in this home, and in 1977, it would erupt in a strange, spectacular, and completely unexpected way. It was on the evening of August 30th, 1977 that Ms. Hodgson was first alerted that something wasn't quite right. It was Johnny and Janet who began complaining of hearing strange knocking sounds on the walls, and even incidents in which the furniture—including the bed—seemed to move by itself. Or as little Janet put it at the time, "The bed was going all funny."

Whatever it was seemed to cease entirely as soon as Peggy walked into the room. Just like a monster that scurries back into the closet as soon as the worried parent arrives on the scene, this poltergeist made itself scarce as soon as mommy Hodgson showed up. But it wouldn't be parent-shy for long. The following night Peggy once again heard the kids complaining of strange sounds and movement; she went up to the bedroom and was told that the chair had moved by itself.

In order to satisfy her children's concerns, Peggy opted to simply take the chair out of the room. She thought perhaps this would put a stop to their overactive imaginations. But it was just a short time later that the poltergeist would rear its ugly head in front of Peggy herself. For she too began hearing the very same strange sounds that her kids were talking about. She heard knocking, scraping, and the sound of furniture being moved—and it seemed to be coming from Johnny and Janet's room.

Suspecting that perhaps her kids were behind the disturbance, Peggy went up to take a look. But upon entering their room she found the children asleep in bed—*yet the noise continued.* Even with them fast asleep, she heard the sound of someone knocking on the wall. Not sure what was going on, Peggy switched on a light. It was as soon as she turned on the light that the poltergeist decided to show itself.

For it was with the bedroom fully lit, that a heavy dresser suddenly sailed across the floor, and stopped in the middle of the room. Peggy was of course, startled, but she managed to temporarily hold off her fears, and instead simply tried to push the dresser back from where it had dislodged itself. But when she pressed against it, she felt as if some unseen force was holding it firmly in place.

It was at this point that she came to the stunning realization that something highly unusual was occurring in her home. Absolutely terrified, she gathered up all of her kids and literally fled the house. Although it was late, they were able to get their surprised neighbors—Vic and Peggy Nottingham—to open their doors and were permitted to stay with them for the night.

Vic and Peggy in the meantime agreed to take a look at the Hodgson home. It seemed that they were under the impression that the Hodgson's had an intruder—an intruder of the human kind that is. Upon venturing into that Enfield home, they too could hear the distinct sound of something banging on the walls. Although they could hear the racket, they could not determine its source.

Unsure of what else to do, they decided to call the police. It was then that Constable Carolyn Keeps came into the picture. Ms. Keeps was a no-nonsense

British police officer, and she would tell it as she saw it. And when she supposedly saw a chair move a few feet across the floor, all of its own accord—she didn't hesitate to report it. Here is her report of what transpired that evening in full:

On Thursday, September 1st, 1977, at approximately 1 am., I was on duty in my capacity as a policewoman, when I received a radio message to 284 Green Street, Enfield. I went to this address where I found a number of people standing in the living room. I was told by the occupier of this house that strange things had been happening during the last few nights and that they believed that the house was haunted. I and another PC entered the living room of the house and the occupier switched off the lights. Almost immediately, I heard the sound of knocking on the wall that backs onto the next-door neighbor's house. There were four distinct taps on the wall and then silence. About two minutes later, I heard more tapping, but this time, it was coming from a different wall, and again it was a distinctive peal of four taps. The lights in the living room were switched off again and within a few minutes, the eldest son pointed to a chair that was standing next to the sofa. I looked at the chair and noticed that it was wobbling slightly from side to side. I then saw the chair slide across the floor towards the kitchen wall. It moved approximately 3 to 4 feet and then came to rest. At no time did it appear to leave the floor. I checked the chair but could find nothing to explain how it had moved. The lights were switched back on. Nothing else happened that night, although we have later reports of disturbances at this address."

This police report provides a stunning testimony from a professional in law enforcement. And this would not be the first time that police would be involved in this case. And just a short time later, a certain Sergeant Brian Hyams, was alerted by a neighbor of this Enfield house, that something really strange was going on at the residence. Hyams arrived on the scene accompanied by another police officer. These two officers clearly could hear audible banging and knocking sounds throughout the home, even though Peggy was the only person in the house at the time.

And as she was under the observation of the officers, there was no way that she could have been running around all over the house pretending to be a ghost rattling the rafters. And if they weren't convinced by the auditory phenomenon, these officers would soon get an eyeful as well, because before their very eyes they began to see items around the house lift up off the ground, defy gravity, and float through the air. And of these objects, the poltergeist seemed to have an especial affinity for Lego.

Or as Hyams later described it, "Lego bricks just started to levitate, or move about I should say, jump about like jumping beans." Hyams then went on to add, "There was a bird in a cage that started squawking. And suddenly, one or two Lego bricks started to fly towards us."

The situation sounds rather bizarre and frightening, and these two veteran officers were apparently frightened enough by it that they, quickly found the exit and took off. Indicating how honest this officer is, he openly admitted to fleeing the scene. Hyams stated, "I'm no hero. I went straight out of the door and I think there was a rush between us who got out the swiftest."

There is no doubt about it, these officers were scared at what they saw. And anyone who has experienced the paranormal firsthand could hardly blame them. Just about anyone would be frightened to see an object suddenly rise up into the air and float in front of them. It's in our nature to be fearful of the unknown. We humans—who have made ourselves the top dogs here on planet Earth—when we are unable to control our surroundings, we do indeed tend to become a bit frightened.

It was after the police ran out of the house that they came across two employees for the *Daily Mirror*—photojournalist Graham Morris and journalist Douglas Bence. The word had apparently gone out as to what was happening in this Enfield home. These two reporters had actually been by on one previous occasion but had not noticed anything unusual.

It was after hearing of the police officer's strange account, however, that they decided that they would go back in. Perhaps feeling encouraged by the power of numbers, the police agreed to escort them, and all four individuals proceeded to enter the residence to brave yet another encounter with the unknown. Photojournalist Graham Morris immediately set up shop with his equipment, but just as this gutsy photographer was getting ready to take some pictures, the poltergeist decided to intervene.

Or as Morris later recalled, "I saw the Lego pieces flying about and I was hit on the head by a piece while I was attempting to photograph it in flight." The man was being attacked by Lego. As ridiculous as it all sounds, poltergeists are not usually too keen to have their activity captured on film, and will indeed try to interfere with any attempt to do so. And he wasn't just hit lightly by a Lego brick—he was hit *hard*. Morris later reported, "I had a bump on my forehead after the incident."

Even so, Morris had the flying Lego brick right in view prior to being struck, and according to him, he should have had it captured on film. But as we shall see in some of the other cases in this book—these poltergeist tricksters somehow have an uncanny knack for preventing the recovery of solid evidence of their happenings. It sounds entirely absurd, but after Morris had his film developed, the section of the photo where a flying Lego brick should have been appearing as just a big blurry "hole" of nothing in the frame.

Is the intelligence behind poltergeist activity able to reach right into the film of a camera and destroy evidence of its existence? As we will see later on in this book—due to repeated incidents like this—such theories have indeed been seriously considered. The strange activity would continue and new witnesses would emerge. For it was on the 4th of September that year, that Bob Richardson, the 72-year-old father of the Hodgson neighbor Mrs. Nottingham, would pay a visit to the Enfield house, and see for himself what all the strange talk was all about.

According to him, it didn't take long for normally inanimate objects to suddenly move of their own accord. Mr. Richardson would report that "two marbles passed me at terrific speed and hit the bathroom floor. When I picked them up, they were hot." The phenomenon of poltergeist-affected objects becoming extremely hot is indeed a known side effect of poltergeist activity. And was frequent at the Enfield haunting.

The police and the reporters, also concurred that the Lego that was hurled at them, were indeed, also quite hot to the touch after they had been thrown by this unseen force. Another British paper the *Daily Mail* got involved in the meantime. The *Daily Mail,* of course, is well known for its penchant for sensational reporting, and the *Daily Mail* of the 1970s was no different.

But it was the folks down at the *Daily Mirror* that decided to really conduct a serious investigation, by sending a veteran, investigative journalist by the name of George Fallowes. Mr. Fallowes was immediately impressed by this story, and realizing that this case was bigger than just some tabloid scoop, he got a hold of what was then the preeminent group of paranormal researchers in the land—*the Society for Psychical Research.*

This group dedicated to psychic, spiritual, and paranormal happenings, was actually founded in the late 1800s and has since been dedicated to using fact-based research into the realm of the paranormal. As it pertains to the Hodgkin's poltergeist, it was lead SPR (Society for Psychical Research) paranormal investigator, Maurice Grosse who was dispatched to the Enfield home on the 5th, of September, in 1977.

Grosse was a veteran researcher, who had spent his early life in business before getting involved with the Society for Psychical Research. He accredited the wealth he had accumulated in his early career, as being able to help finance his endeavors with SPR. Upon his entrance into the Hodgson home, Grosse found a family that was understandably disturbed. He did his best, however, to assure them that poltergeist phenomena are more common than people realize and that as frightening as the activity may be, it is almost always short-term in duration.

Mr. Grosse's calm, confident reassurance seemed to greatly soothe the family's rattled nerves. He not only believed their story but described the bizarre happenings almost as if they were natural (natural as in, having a natural known pattern), if not extraordinary events. Hurricanes and meteor showers after all are natural, but incredibly devastating all the same. Particularly soothing for Mrs. Hodgson, was

Grosse's suggestion that she journals what transpired in the home.

It seems that keeping a record of the events, not only helped to clarify what was happening but seemed to give Mrs. Hodgson some semblance of power and control. She was now not just a hapless victim—she herself was also a researcher tracking and examining these incredible events.

Interestingly enough, it was upon Maurice Grosse's entrance onto the scene, that the activity seemed to briefly die down. In the first few days of his investigation, not much happened, except for the nightly banging on walls, which continued on a regular basis. It was on September 8th however, that Mr. Grosse would experience a sudden uptick in the poltergeist phenomenon. For it was shortly after 1 in the morning on that day, that Mr. Grosse, along with news reporters and photographers who had camped out for the evening—heard a tremendous bang—significantly louder than all the rest, in Janet and Johnny's room.

They all ran to see what had been the source of the sound, and upon entry, they saw that a large, heavy chair, had traveled across the room, and apparently slammed into the wall on the other side. Neither Janet nor her sickly brother Johnny should have been able to hurl this heavy chair. Furthermore, the kids weren't even awake.

Shortly thereafter, one of the photojournalists could have sworn he saw the chair move by itself. He took a picture, but since the photo was unable to capture any movement—as far as evidence of the paranormal goes—this lone photo of a chair doesn't accomplish too much. The following night saw the more paranormal phenomenon, including marbles seen hurling across the room by themselves, as well as dresser drawers opening of their own volition.

Investigators Maurice Grosse and the journalists who accompanied him, however, camped out to see what new things they could figure out about the strange happenings. It was around 10 o'clock that evening that Maurice claims he himself witnessed a marble suddenly go airborne, and shoot right by him, apparently all of its own accord. The group then witnessed door chimes seeming to sway back and forth, with no apparent cause for the movement.

Another investigator was then spooked by what they witnessed in the bathroom and hurriedly called Maurice to come to take a look. As Maurice stood by, he claims to have witnessed the door open and close by itself several times. Maurice then went to the kitchen, where he witnessed a shirt lift up from a "pile of clothes" and land on the kitchen table, before sliding off the table and coming to rest on the ground.

A little later, Grosse saw more marbles spontaneously go flying, some of them apparently aimed at Janet. It was then that he made an astute observation. He noticed that the marbles once airborne, rather than hitting the ground and rolling to a stop--they seemed to instantly become motionless as soon as they hit the ground.

This unusual feature would seem to defy the known laws of physics. Under normal conditions if a person had thrown a marble, you would expect the marble to hit the ground, perhaps bounce a few times, and proceed to roll across the floor until it came to a stop. Yet these poltergeist-tossed marbles came to an uncanny stop as soon as they touched back down on the ground.

This odd fact alone was quite indicative that they were dealing with something that did not operate under the normal laws of physics that the rest of us do. It was also around this time that Maurice Grosse came to the conclusion that it was Janet who was the focal point of poltergeist activity. Not only did marbles fly at her at random, but Maurice also noticed other objects suddenly come to life, as soon as Janet walked by.

On September 9th, Richardson also noticed a connection with Janet, yet even when she was far away, the activity continued. Richardson was near a goldfish tank when the lid of the tank suddenly flew off and landed on the floor. Janet, who felt like folks were blaming her for the mischief, was on the other side of the house when the incident occurred. And took note of this fact, by stating, "Well, I didn't do that, did I?"

No—although she was somehow a focus of activity, it became clear that she was not consciously causing the activity to occur. It was the following day that this Enfield home besieged with the paranormal managed to make its way to the cover of copies of the *Daily Mirror* which introduced the poltergeist case as simply "The House of Strange Happenings."

This piece introduced a larger audience to the "strange happenings" at the house in Enfield, and soon other media outlets were calling. A British-based TV series called "Night Line" did a segment on it, and the BBC also covered the story. By September 20th, in the meantime, more strange events were noted by the investigators and journalists present.

A book was supposedly seen suddenly launching itself off of a mantle, sailing through an open door, and then crashing into the closed door of a room immediately across the way. Making it even creepier, the book that caused the mischief, was a tome entitled *Fun and Games for Children.* That same night a large dresser was seen falling over by itself, prompting the eldest child in the Hodgson household—13-year-old Margaret to exclaim, "Whatever it is—it's bloody powerful!"

It was the evening after this incident, that paranormal investigator Maurice Grosse, saw another inexplicable event—this one a bit more whimsical than the last. For instead of just hurling books or knocking over furniture—he saw an inanimate object do a "little dance" for him. He was taking a break in the kitchen, when a teapot on the counter near the stove, suddenly rose up, and like some kind of tea-time, marionette swayed back and forth as if it was dancing. Or as Maurice described it at the time, it was "doing a little dance right in front of my eyes."

It became clear to those involved that they desperately needed to get some of this paranormal activity documented on tape. This led to cameras being installed at various points throughout the house, in the hope that they might pick up on something. If a camera is pointed at the dancing teapot, it should pick up the action, right? But as we will learn—failure to do this is an aspect somehow common in these cases. The intelligence behind the phenomena seemed to know what the investigators were trying to do, and was determined to thwart their efforts.

Inexplicably, as soon as cameras were put up, they began to have technical problems, rendering them completely useless. Even expensive motion-detecting cameras that were designed to capture anything that was to suddenly move in front of them, were found to repeatedly have dead batteries, despite being fully charged before being turned on. And as you might have guessed, this trickster poltergeist was sure to engage in prolific paranormal antics as soon as the camera's batteries were safely dead, and the camera inoperable.

Yet, just as mysteriously, as soon as malfunctioning equipment was taken out of the Hodgson's home, they worked just fine. Interestingly, however, as much as the Hodgson house was the obvious epicenter of activity, there were occasions in which the poltergeist phenomena would spill over into the homes of their neighbors.

Janet, Margaret, and Billy at one point were shuffled off to Peggy's brother John Burcombe's house, who lived nearby. Here the paranormal activity continued and some of it was witnessed by Mr. Burcombe. At one point, he saw a large TV move by itself, a lamp also moved, and on at least one occasion, he saw a drawer suddenly open of its own volition. In describing his reaction to these strange events, Mr. Burcombe didn't hide his fear—using British vernacular for being scared witless, he exclaimed that he was "bloody petrified."

Since the activity appeared to follow Janet to the Burcombe home, it was clear that she was indeed the focal point of this poltergeist maelstrom. And as much as the activity was drawn to her, it would soon turn on her in a downright violent fashion. It's said that back at the Hodgson's home, a curtain that was near Janet at the time, suddenly curled up into a kind of rope, and almost succeeded in coiling right around Janet's throat—as if it wanted to choke her.

The most infamous phenomenon, in this case, occurred a short time later, however, when the poltergeist appeared to make Janet "levitate." Janet's alleged levitation was supposedly seen by a neighbor who was walking by the house and happened to glance in the window and saw Janet floating off her bed. Skeptics have suggested however that perhaps Janet was actually jumping on the bed and the neighbor only happened to see the brief jump. It seems a bit hard to believe, however, that someone could confuse the obvious movement of jumping with outright levitation.

The most infamous aspect of this case is that there is an alleged photo that one of the "automatic cameras" captured of Janet—floating. In the image, she is almost near the ceiling, appearing to have been flung right off the bed. Skeptics of course would say that she just jumped, but by looking at the image of the supposed event, she doesn't *look* like she jumped, since she appears to be in a sitting position and *not a jumping position.* It's this photo that makes one successful documentation of this alleged poltergeist so spooky.

If such a photo was taken today, it would probably be debunked as being photoshopped. But since this incident dates back to the 1970s, this of course is not possible. The only explanations are, either she somehow managed to jump in an extremely awkward fashion, or she really did float up into the air. She also had her mother as a nearby witness, and she steadfastly testified that Janet was indeed seen levitating up off of the bed. At the time, Ms. Hodgson clearly stated, "Janet was lying in bed and I was talking to Janet. Janet was suddenly flying through the air."

This poltergeist haunting would ultimately reach its climax in December of 1977 when auditory projections began to emerge. Auditory sounds (other than knocking and banging) were noticeably absent in the beginning. But just like the Bell Witch and other supposed poltergeist cases, someone or *something* seemed like it was getting ready to verbally communicate.

At first, those at the Enfield house began to hear "barking" and "whistling" noises. These sounds eventually evolved into words—words produced by what has been described as an "old" and "raspy" voice. Investigators carried on conversations with this voice, which claimed to be someone named "Joe Watson."

It's important to note, that just because the poltergeist suggested it had an identity and was named Joe Watson, this does not mean that the entity was telling the truth. These trickster entities are known to lie and invent whole backstories for themselves that are complete fabrications. One poltergeist might say they're a mongoose, another a witch, and another might even present a full-blown name for itself—but none of it is necessarily real.

The poltergeist in the Enfield case—as poltergeists are known to do—soon changed its backstory and said that its name was actually "Bill." Part of the controversy in the Enfield case is that while the voice at times seemed to come from odd locations in the house, such as under Janet's bed—at other times it seemed to come from Janet herself. Was the entity speaking through Janet? Or was she simply a gifted ventriloquist and impersonator pulling everyone's leg?

This part of the case still sparks quite a bit of debate. But if anyone were to search for the recordings made of this voice (and yes, this time around, some of it was indeed caught on tape), most agree that they are quite disturbing. Maurice Grosse for his part was a believer and claimed that no young girl like Janet could have impersonated the low gravelly voice that was emanating from the Enfield home.

And furthermore, he argued that even if it were possible, doing such a thing for hours on end—as the poltergeist did—would have severely strained and damaged Janet's vocal cords. Yet while all of this was going on, Janet's normal high-pitched voice, remained unaffected and under no apparent strain whatsoever. The events would slowly die down in 1978 and finally, end completely in 1979.

The lengthy duration of this case is unusual. As mentioned earlier in this chapter, and as was pointed out by paranormal researcher Maurice Grosse, many poltergeist cases are much shorter in duration. Most last for a month or two at most—but Janet's poltergeist lasted for two years. This was indeed an extraordinary case, and the merits of it are still hotly debated.

Renate Beck and the Indianapolis Poltergeist

In the Spring of 1962, a single mother Renate Beck, and her daughter—13-year-old Linda—began to experience strange happenings in their home. They lived in an otherwise quiet neighborhood in Indianapolis, Indiana when the poltergeist activity began to occur that March.

At the outset of the activity, Renate began waking up with strange bites on her body. Now, waking up with bites does not of course, necessarily mean that one has a poltergeist on their hands.

Bites could occur from the common mosquito—or for those who are much less fortunate—even bed bugs. But Renate Beck was not being bitten by any known critter from the animal kingdom. Although she described the bites as being akin to "bat bites" they didn't exactly correspond with a bat's mouth either. The bites were huge, and menacing-looking and no one knew what to make of them.

The bites were also accompanied by odd noises in the middle of the night, and the sudden destruction of fragile items around the home. According to Renate, it was while all of these bumps in the night were taking place, that she "felt the sting on her left arm" and after examining herself in the light, discovered that she had these horrendous bites up and down her arm. And she wasn't the only one.

Also afflicted were her mother, Lina Gemmecke, and her daughter Linda. A paranormal investigator by the name of William G. Roll was contacted shortly after the news story broke, and investigated the premises. He investigated the damage to the property, as well as the visible marks left behind on the residents, and was intrigued by the case. After talking to Renate, Mr. Roll learned that she had recently witnessed clear poltergeist activity firsthand.

It was on the morning of March 10th, when Renate was simply having a cup of coffee with her mother, when she bore witness to a cup rising up off the kitchen counter and sail clear across the kitchen, only to slam into the kitchen wall. Both women witnessed this bizarre and startling event. Renate Beck's mind immediately turned to the supernatural, and due to her belief that perhaps the spirits of those who had passed could be trying to make their presence known, she considered the date—March 10th.

As it turns out, March 10th was her father's date of birth. The thing is, neither Renate nor her mother knew whether her Dad was alive or dead. Her mother—a German immigrant—had separated from the man while she was still in Germany, some 20 years prior. No one knew his whereabouts, but since the strange happenings began on his birthday, Renate openly speculated that perhaps her Dad had since passed and he was trying to reach out to her from beyond the grave.

It was a short time after this event, that both Renate and her mother suddenly felt a stabbing pain in their arms, and looked down to see more bite marks. The bites would sporadically continue in the coming days—some of them witnessed by paranormal investigator William G. Roll himself. One interesting fact that William G. Roll noticed early on in this case, was that Renate's daughter Linda appeared to be immune to the bites.

While Renate and Linda's grandmother were being bitten left and right—Linda herself was not being bothered at all. He also noted that Renate's mother, Mrs. Gemmecke, seemed to suffer from the bites more than her daughter, with the activity seemingly centered primarily around her. Although Mrs. Gemmecke herself tried to dismiss the happenings as merely "spider bites" Mr. Roll knew that she did not really believe this, as she appeared quite spooked by the happenings and even resorted to using the "sign of the cross" to ward off something she apparently felt was much more troubling than mere spiders.

Mrs. Gemmecke would suffer yet another severe biting attack on March 18th, even sustaining vampire-like bite marks on her chest. The bites seemed to subside shortly thereafter, however, replaced by a new—yet more familiar poltergeist phenomenon—random knocking on the walls of the home. The knocking and banging sounds seemed to first emerge on March 18th. Mr. Roll was present for some of this activity and openly speculated that perhaps some neighborhood kids were playing a prank on them.

Nevertheless, the knocking continued and no pranksters ever turned up. Mrs. Gemmecke's' mental state began to greatly decline at this point. And she actually began to long for her native Germany. She apparently began to even somehow blame her adopted country for the happenings. In a moment of frustration, she was heard declaring, "Ist Amerika verhekst? So war es nie in Deutschland!" Which roughly translated means, "Is America hexed/cursed? It wasn't like this in Germany!"

It's ironic of course, that a German-speaking woman, would accuse America as being the cursed land of the "poltergeist" since the phenomenon—as indicated by its German name—had indeed been known to occur in *Deutschland* as well! Mrs. Gemmecke's mental state didn't improve after this, and after the evening of March 22nd, she had a particularly rough time.

It was after a spate of several paranormal happenings, in which the walls were pounded with knocks, and objects moved of their own accord, that Renate found her mother—oddly enough—passed out in a closet. Even more bizarre, the woman didn't have any clothes on. In Mr. Roll's report on this matter, he doesn't quite explain why this is the case—but apparently, this was indeed how Renate found her mother that day.

Mrs. Gemmecke was apparently writhing around stark naked in a state of hysteria, as she shouted over and over, "The devils are here! The devils are here!" Mrs. Gemmecke became more and more out of control at this point, and eventually, Renate had to call the police on her own mother.

Mrs. Gemmecke was ultimately charged with "disorderly conduct." Seeing Mrs. Gemmecke hauled away in handcuffs led many in the community to speculate that it was perhaps Mrs. Gemmecke that was the source of the problem all along. Shortly after she made bail, she was fed up with it all, and decided to get on a plane and go back to Germany. She left on March 31st. The poltergeist activity ceased after her departure.

Poltergeists and Skinwalkers

In Native American lore, a "Skinwalker" is a supernatural shapeshifter. At least in some instances, according to Native American tradition, it is a human who initiates the Skinwalker process. Just imagine a shaman walking around with a wolf skin on his back, preparing to actually transform into the beast, and you get the idea. But the legend of the Skinwalker is more than about a mere human—even a human who has developed supernatural abilities—but also pertains to entities that are definitely *not human*, yet still interact with our world.

In many ways, the Skinwalker of Native American lore had attributes and manifested phenomena that are very similar to what would otherwise be termed poltergeists. By and large, the notion of Skinwalkers came to the wider world's attention in the 1990s through a family whose name has come down to us as the "Shermans." They bought a ranch in a quiet, rural corner of the Uinta Basin region of northeastern Utah, on land which local Native Americans long claimed was cursed by the Skinwalkers.

After settling into the ranch, the Shermans soon had to agree with this. For not long after their arrival, very strange things began to occur around the property. They would hear random banging and knock at night, and these sounds soon evolved into disembodied voices. Such things, of course, are classic hallmarks of a poltergeist. But the Sherman household at

Skinwalker Ranch experienced a much stranger phenomenon—even stranger than what's normally reported in your typical poltergeist case.

They saw orbs of light, strange shadowy entities, and even more distressing for this ranger family—their livestock suffered from periodic cattle mutilations. They also saw what they termed to be UFOs which were allegedly seen coming through "portals" that would randomly open on the horizon.

They supposedly saw a wide range of UFO vehicles, from "football field-sized" craft, to odd, small "box-like" craft, that looked somewhat reminiscent of an elongated refrigerator, which would defy gravity and hover over the ground with no obvious source of propulsion.

In the midst of all of this paranormal activity, the family finally reached breaking point, when they believed that the aforementioned floating orbs had "disintegrated" their dogs. The dogs had chased after the balls of light, and a yelp, and a sizzle later, the Shermans ran out to find nothing left of the canines but piles of greasy liquid. Although no one can really prove it (it's possible the dogs just ran off) the Shermans insist that these smokey piles of grease were all that remained of their dogs.

Fearing for the physical safety of his own family, Mr. Sherman finally decided to sell the ranch. It was bought in 1996 by billionaire and paranormal guru Robert Bigelow. Bigelow had heard of the frightening happenings at the ranch and rather than running from it—*he ran to it.* He set up a 24-hour research station in fact, with scientists posted on every corner, and more importantly—*cameras running 24 hours a day/7 days a week.* So, they must have captured some great footage, right?

Unfortunately, the answer to that question is a resounding *no*. So, did they decide the whole thing was a hoax? Absolutely not! They became true believers! The scientists who worked at the ranch all came away with their belief in undoubtedly paranormal encounters. They saw things there that defied explanation. They saw the UFOs and they even saw the supposed "interdimensional portals" Mr. Sherman had witnessed. And even more bizarre, on one occasion, researchers equipped with night vision goggles even bore witness to what they could only describe as a classic "Bigfoot" type creature.

They claim to have seen this portal opens up on a distant part of the ranch with their own eyes. The portal opened—and the next thing these stunned observers knew, a bigfoot dropped out, and took off running. The crazy thing about the ranch though, is that whatever intelligence was behind the phenomena clearly did not want any of these manifestations captured on film.

As was the case in the Enfield haunting, all cameras posted at Skinwalker Ranch malfunctioned and became inoperable whenever the manifestations occurred. Not only that, in one ominous instance, one camera, situated up high on a pole, was found to be deliberately sabotaged, with heavy wiring, literally ripped out of it. Oddly enough, there was a camera pointed directly at this sabotaged camera which should have picked up the other camera's destruction.

Yet upon replaying the film (and this camera did indeed keep filming) at the moment that the other camera went out, and something should have been seen ripping the guts out of it—the footage of the still operable camera shows absolutely *nothing* taking place. Just a camera mounted on a distant pole, with absolutely nothing happening. Yet this obviously wasn't the case for the folks on the ground, who could look up and see the demolished camera right in front of them.

It was as if, this entity—this unseen force—could somehow manipulate reality itself. The camera was obviously destroyed, yet the film of the other camera shows an alternative reality in which the camera was not destroyed and nothing happened.
The scientists at the ranch found themselves in a cat-and-mouse game with the unseen force at the ranch, in which it was somehow always one step ahead of them.

Try as they might, after several years' worth of attempts, they could not capture much of anything significant on film. But the fact that we have a small army of scientific researchers swearing that they saw incredible events occur, and real-world artifacts such as cameras that were damaged by an unseen force, testifies that something was indeed happening at Skinwalker Ranch.

Interestingly enough, it has also recently come to light that these manifestations at the ranch would come to individually haunt many of the researchers involved. They would later admit that poltergeist activity actually followed them back to their homes. Yes, even once they were away from this haunted ranch, once they were back in the safety of their homes, similar odd events would start manifesting on their own personal property. It didn't matter where they lived, they could depart from that poltergeist-infested Utah ranch, and head back to an apartment in New York City—and still, the odd happenings would follow them.

The Skinwalker Ranch is a complex case that crosses many paranormal thresholds, but it's worth noting that there was a heavy UFO element at the ranch, with craft frequently seen coming out of those so-called interdimensional portals. Having that said, it's worth mentioning that the UFO/ET phenomenon also comes with a poltergeist element attached to it. Many who encounter UFOs/ETs have claimed that they were plagued with odd paranormal activity after encountering them, such as objects moving about their house, or odd sound effects occurring.

The late great UFO researcher John Keel once dubbed this effect "high strangeness." One of the most famous UFO experiencers to claim to have been subjected to this *high strangeness* was none other than Betty Hill. Betty and her husband Barney Hill were traveling down a lonely stretch of road one night in the 1960s when they were allegedly intercepted by a UFO whose alien occupants forced them onto their craft.

Here they underwent what is now the classic alien abduction narrative—of being medically examined by ET entities, before being returned to their car. This story, of course, is startling enough as it is, but in later years Betty would admit that along with the actual alien abduction experience, she and Barney also went through poltergeist-like activity after the encounter. Or as Keel called it, "high strangeness."

This high strangeness is actually a fairly common after-effect in purported ET encounters. One theory that has been presented as to why this might be actually dovetailed quite nicely into one of the most generally accepted theories as it pertains to the poltergeist phenomenon. For there are some ufologists who have suggested that the odd happenings in post-alien abduction cases are actually being caused by the alleged abductees themselves.

Just as is typical in your standard poltergeist account, it's believed that the mind of alien abductees is so stressed and supercharged, that's it's actually their own subconscious mind which is causing objects to levitate, and weird sounds to manifest. All of this occurs on a subconscious level, so that the frightened individual, doesn't even know that they are doing it.

But why would an encounter with a UFO cause someone's psyche to become so hyper-charged that poltergeist activity would emerge? Some have speculated that ET's might use an advanced technology that couples itself with the power of the mind, and it is their advanced psionic technology that causes side effects on us hapless humans. Pretty far-fetched sure, but according to UFO lore, ET craft is indeed full of all sorts of tech that blends mind and machine together.

The Skinwalker Ranch is said to have had a heavy UFO element, and some have theorized that the region itself serves as an interdimensional portal that this craft regularly pop in and out from (bigfoots apparently like to pop out of them too) and if that's the case, maybe all of this activity keeps the ranch—as well as anyone who happens across it—in a hyper-charged psychic state.

For it must be noted, that as paranormally active as the Skinwalker Ranch is, the one classic poltergeist puzzle piece that seems to be missing, is the "focus" of the poltergeist events. Usually, there is one person on which the poltergeist activity is focused. In the Enfield case, it was young Janet for example, that seemed to be the focus of the phenomena. At the Skinwalker Ranch, however, there is no individual focus—people come and people go—yet the activity remains.

As crazy as all of this stuff sounds, it would be really nice to write it off as fiction, but the odd events of

Skinwalker Ranch have led to some real-world developments. It's said that some of Bigelow's findings actually influenced the U.S. government's investigation into UAPs (Unidentified Aerial Phenomenon). The Pentagon apparently took a good hard look at poltergeist phenomena in conjunction with UFOs, and even coined their own phrase for those who have UFO encounters and "take something home with them." It's reported that back at the Pentagon they were referring to these tag-along poltergeists as "hitchhikers."

But even if we can theorize a connection between UFO activity and poltergeist activity, this is not to say that UFOs are the direct cause of poltergeists entirely. There was certainly no UFO present over John Bell's farm during the Bell Witch incident. The larger truth that some researchers have come to grasp, is that poltergeists are most likely naturally occurring psychic phenomenon among human beings, which can occasionally be triggered.

Much of the time poltergeists are triggered by a young adolescent, under a lot of stress, causing them to subconsciously manifest poltergeist events. As it pertains to UFOs then, if they are not the origin of the poltergeist, perhaps there is something about UFOs that can trigger them within people.

If it's not UFO mind-melding machine technology that is triggering the poltergeist response, some have pointed out that it could simply be the terrible fear and stress provoked by ET encounters themselves that triggers folks to exhibit poltergeist symptoms.

That would actually make a lot of sense if one is to subscribe to the poltergeist theory that poltergeist events are brought about by deeply distressed individuals whose anxiety manifests through the poltergeist phenomenon.

Because what, after all, could be more stressful than randomly being picked up off the side of the road by a bunch of bug-eyed aliens? These strange connections that have inspired a range of theories as it pertains to poltergeist activity, certainly do make one stop and wonder.

One Noisy Ghost

Many of us can probably recall a time when we were children and found ourselves fixated on an inanimate object such as a stuffed animal or action figure. Perhaps we stared at our teddy bear and imagined what it would be like if it were to suddenly move. The more we thought about it—the more it seemed possible. Watching that teddy in the dim light of our bedroom, in our mind we may have even convinced ourselves that it did slightly move, just as we were about to drift off to sleep.

The minds of youngsters tend to be more open to such things than adults, and perhaps this is the reason why it is typically around young people that poltergeist phenomena usually manifest.

Their minds are like tuning forks, and on some rare occasions are able to use their imagination not to just pretend fantastical things are happening, but to actually *make fantastic things happen.*

Most paranormal researchers who have looked into poltergeist cases like those mentioned in this book are convinced that poltergeists are indeed the product of the subconscious mind. The human mind is indeed probably more powerful than we realize. It's often said that we only ever use a small fraction of our potential brainpower within our lifetime. Could it be that all of that latent untapped potential has the capacity to manipulate matter—maybe even reality itself? If only we knew how to harness it?

The keyword there is "harness" since poltergeist activity if we do indeed believe it to be unconscious psychic projections from the human mind, is the opposite of a controlled and harnessed phenomenon. On the contrary, these uncontrollable maelstroms of psychic power are entirely unpredictable and uncontrollable. It's certainly an interesting theory to consider poltergeists as being an unregulated burst of psychic activity from the subconscious human mind, but that's not the only explanation that has been offered.

Another, the perhaps more disturbing theory is that maybe poltergeists are not produced by human beings at all—not even on an unconscious level—but are the result of some unknown intelligence that occasionally penetrates into our reality. This theory postulates that it is the unknown intelligence that picks on and uses individual humans as a conduit in which to focus its powers, but that the actual intelligence behind the poltergeist is completely independent of their human host.

The events of the Skinwalker Ranch seem to lend credence to this theory since as it pertains to the poltergeist activity, in this case, there is no single person that the activity centers around. Instead of focusing on one individual, the unseen force at the ranch is said to focus on anyone and everyone who is around.

One thing that is clear, whether poltergeists are psychic creations of human beings, or independent entities of their own—they are notorious liars. As the cases presented in this book can attest, whatever a poltergeist claims to be its origin or backstory, you can almost guarantee that it will be proven false.

Poltergeists that have reached the level of being able to speak, are notorious tricksters and absolutely thrive on deception. They also don't like to be caught on camera. All of the cases of poltergeists destroying cameras and other electronic equipment make clear that whatever a poltergeist is, they don't want to reveal themselves.

So, the enigma remains. If you do, however, ever happen to see a cup float across the room, followed by the voice of a talking mongoose—please do take note. Because whatever may be behind these troublesome, noisy ghosts—you are almost certainly in for quite a show!

Further Readings

In this section, you will find a list of suggested further readings and reference materials.

Poltergeists and Other Hauntings. Rupert Mathews
Mr. Mathews presents a wide variety of poltergeist cases. His theories and findings were helpful for this text.

The Poltergeist. William G. Roll
William G. Roll is a dynamic figure in the field of poltergeists, and this book showcases some of his most important cases.

Poltergeists: Examining Mysteries of the Paranormal. Michael Clarkson
This is an excellent anthology on the poltergeist phenomenon and does a good job at presenting some of the more modern cases.

www.mysteriousuniverse.org
This site specializes in all things paranormal and some of the latest findings on the connection between poltergeists, the Skinwalker Ranch, and the Pentagon's study on UAPs, can be found here.

Printed in Great Britain
by Amazon